National Military Strategy to Combat Weapons of Mass Destruction

13 February 2006
Chairman of the Joint Chiefs of Staff
Washington, DC 20318

TABLE OF CONTENTS

SECRETARY'S FOREWORD... 2

CHAIRMAN'S MEMORANDUM... 3

EXECUTIVE SUMMARY.. 4

CHAPTER 1: INTRODUCTION.. 9

CHAPTER 2: GUIDING PRINCIPLES 13

CHAPTER 3: STRATEGIC MILITARY FRAMEWORK........................ 16

CHAPTER 4: OPERATIONAL GUIDANCE 20

CHAPTER 5: CONCLUSION 28

ANNEX A: TERMS & DEFINITIONS.. 29

Foreword

Weapons of mass destruction (WMD) pose a serious threat to the United States and the international community. In the hands of our adversaries, these weapons could enable them to inflict massive harm on the United States, including our military forces at home and abroad, and our friends and allies. The cost of insufficient preparation against such an attack would be substantial.

Since September 11, 2001, the Department of Defense has made progress, but more remains to be done to combat WMD. This document, the National Military Strategy to Combat Weapons of Mass Destruction, outlines the Department's approach in fulfilling its role in implementing the President's vision for the protection of the United States, our forces, and our friends and allies from the existing and growing WMD threat. It complements the three pillars of combating WMD as set forth in the National Strategy to Combat Weapons of Mass Destruction: counterproliferation to combat WMD use, strengthened nonproliferation to combat WMD proliferation, and consequence management to respond to WMD use.

The National Military Strategy to Combat WMD defines a Strategic Endstate, Military Strategic Objectives, and the missions and means to achieve them. This framework provides the Department a construct on which to base deliberate planning, coordination activities, operations, and capabilities development.

In addition, it concludes that although the Department has an important role to play in combating WMD, we must and will integrate DoD efforts with those of other elements of the U.S. Government, allies, and partners.

I endorse the National Military Strategy to Combat Weapons of Mass Destruction as applicable to the entire Department of Defense.

Donald H. Rumsfeld
Secretary of Defense

CM-0194-06
13 February 2006

MEMORANDUM FOR: Distribution List

Subject: National Military Strategy to Combat Weapons of Mass Destruction
(NMS-CWMD)

1. Our Nation faces an increasing threat from the use of WMD by hostile state
and nonstate actors. The complexity of this threat also increases with the
rapid advance of technologies used to develop and deliver WMD. We must
possess the full range of operational capabilities to protect the United States,
US military forces, and partners and allies from the threat or actual use of
WMD. This strategy provides overarching guidance to help focus military
efforts to accomplish this critical mission.

2. The NMS-CWMD presents the comprehensive, coherent guidance needed to
succeed while executing the US military WMD-related nonproliferation,
counterproliferation, and consequence-management missions. It also provides
strategic guidance for supporting other departments and agencies as directed,
at home and abroad.

3. The keys to successful protection against the threat or use of WMD against
the United States, its interests, partners, and allies are our people and their
dedication to this vital mission. Cohesive operations conducted within the
framework provided by this NMS-CWMD will ensure the members of the US
military are able to operate as a single team and ultimately defeat the efforts of
our enemies.

PETER PACE
General, United States Marine Corps
Chairman
of the Joint Chiefs of Staff

EXECUTIVE SUMMARY

The National Military Strategy (NMS) to Combat Weapons of Mass Destruction (WMD) is derived from the Department of Defense's (DOD) mission to dissuade, deter and defeat those who seek to harm the United States, its allies, and partners through WMD use or threat of use and, if attacked, to mitigate the effects and restore deterrence. Its purpose is to provide DOD Components guidance and a strategic framework for combating WMD. The strategy uses an "ends, ways, means" approach to planning, executing and resourcing, and emphasizes those combating WMD missions in which the military plays a prominent role.

Guiding Principles Six guiding principles underpin the National Military Strategy to Combat WMD. These principles should be used as a foundation for the development of all combating WMD concepts of operations and plans. *Active, Layered, Defense-in-Depth.* In order to protect the United States and defeat aggressors, the U.S. Armed Forces must establish an active defense. The U.S. Armed Forces will focus military planning, posture, operations, and capabilities, in accordance with mission essential tasks, on the active, forward and layered defense of our nation, our allies, partners, and interests. *Situational Awareness and Integrated Command and Control.* The decision to employ specialized combating WMD capabilities for simultaneous operations demands a highly flexible and adaptive command and control process informed by timely, credible, and actionable intelligence. *Global Force Management.* Any combating WMD capabilities we develop in the future must be visible to combatant command planners and include responsive and agile forces that can be rapidly task organized and equipped to accomplish assigned missions. *Capabilities-Based Planning.* We must plan for and develop capabilities that could be employed against a range of threats and associated capabilities while balancing the requirements for targeted strategies against known proliferators. *Effects-Based Approach.* We will use an effects-based approach in planning, execution, and assessments to achieve efficient results and reduce risk to mission and campaign objectives, as well as to our combating WMD-related resources. *Assurance.* Where possible, we will encourage action by like-minded States, work with our international allies, partners, and operate through regional States to combat WMD actively.

> **Six Guiding Principles**
>
> Active, Layered, Defense-in-Depth
> Situational Awareness and Integrated Command and Control
> Global Force Management
> Capabilities-Based Planning
> Effects-Based Approach
> Assurance

Strategic Military Framework The strategic military framework to combat WMD consists of *ends* (the military strategic goal and associated end state), *ways* (military strategic objectives), and *means* (combatant commands, Military Departments, and combat support agencies) applied across the three pillars of the *National Strategy to Combat WMD* (nonproliferation, counterproliferation, and consequence management).

Ends (Military Strategic Goal and Associated End state) Our military strategic goal is to ensure that the United States, its Armed Forces, allies, partners, and interests are neither coerced nor attacked by enemies using WMD. Specific end states delineate standards by which we can measure our effectiveness:

1. U.S. Armed Forces, in concert with other elements of U.S. national power, deter WMD use.

2. U. S. Armed Forces are prepared to defeat an adversary threatening to use WMD and prepare to deter follow-on use.

3. Existing worldwide WMD is secure and the U.S. Armed Forces contribute as appropriate to secure, reduce, reverse or eliminate it.

4. Current or potential adversaries are dissuaded from producing WMD.

5. Current or potential adversaries' WMD is detected and characterized and elimination sought.

6. Proliferation of WMD and related materials to current and/or potential adversaries is dissuaded, prevented, defeated or reversed.

7. If WMD is used against the United States or its interests, U.S. Armed Forces are capable of minimizing the effects in order to continue operations in a WMD environment and assist United States civil authorities, allies and partners.

8. U.S Armed Forces assist in attributing the source of attack, respond decisively, and/or deter future attacks.

9. Allies and U.S. civilian agencies are capable partners in combating WMD.

Ways (Military Strategic Objectives) The military strategic objectives (MSOs) are achieved through eight missions conducted across the combating WMD continuum. *Defeat and Deter WMD use and subsequent use.* Adversaries must believe they will suffer severe consequences and that their objectives will be denied if they threaten or resort to the use of WMD. *Protect, Respond and Recover from WMD use.* The purpose of this objective is to respond to an adversary who has used WMD on the battlefield or against strategic U.S.

interests. To protect and recover from WMD use, U.S. Armed Forces will execute passive defense measures and be prepared to conduct WMD consequence management activities. *Defend, Dissuade or Deny WMD proliferation or possession.* To prevent, dissuade or deny adversaries or potential adversaries from possessing or proliferating WMD, U.S. Armed Forces will be prepared to conduct offensive operations. The military must also support interdiction efforts, security cooperation, and nonproliferation efforts.

Military Strategic Objectives
Defeat, Deter Protect, Respond, Recover Defend, Dissuade, Deny Reduce, Destroy, Reverse

Reduce, Destroy or Reverse WMD possession. To reverse WMD programs and reduce WMD and related material stockpiles, the U.S. Armed Forces will support threat reduction cooperation as well as be prepared to assist in cooperative stockpile destruction activities.

Means (Combatant Commands, Military Departments, and Combat Support Agencies). The combatant commands, military departments, and combat support agencies are the means to accomplish MSOs. Commander, U.S. Strategic Command (CDRUSSTRATCOM) is the lead combatant commander for integrating and synchronizing DOD in combating WMD. Consistent with this assignment, USSTRATCOM will integrate and synchronize applicable Department of Defense-wide efforts across the doctrine, organization, training, material, leadership, personnel, and facilities spectrum. Combatant Commanders will continue to execute combating WMD missions within their AORs. Military efforts will need to be integrated with other organizations and nations that possess capabilities, resources, or information that can contribute to the mission.

Strategic Enablers Strategic enablers are crosscutting capabilities that facilitate execution of the military strategy. They enhance the effectiveness and integration of military combating WMD mission capabilities. Commanders must continually assess enabling capabilities and identify required improvements. Three strategic enablers facilitate DoD's efforts to combat  WMD: intelligence, partnership capacity, and strategic communication support. *Intelligence.* Intelligence directly supports strategy, planning, and decision-making; facilitates improvements in operational capabilities; and informs programming and risk management. To reduce uncertainty, our intelligence capability must exploit a variety of sources, facilitate information sharing, and improve situational awareness. *Partnership Capacity.* Building partnership capacity, bilaterally and multilaterally, enhances our capability to combat WMD. We should build on and leverage U.S. Government, Non-Government Organizations, corporate and international partner capability. Security cooperation efforts should not only focus on missile defense cooperation or the Proliferation Security Initiative (PSI), but equally stress passive defense, elimination, and WMD consequence management cooperation. *Strategic Communication Support.* The military plays a significant supporting role in the larger U.S. Government effort to communicate and demonstrate our resolve. Strategic communications shape perceptions at the global, regional, and national levels. U.S. words and actions reassure allies and partners and underscore, to potential adversaries, the costs and risks associated with WMD acquisition and use.

Military Mission Areas The military mission is to dissuade, deter, and defeat those who seek to harm the United States, its allies, and partners through WMD use or threat of use. This mission is in direct support of the three pillars (nonproliferation, counterproliferation, and consequence management) of the national strategy for combating WMD.

Across the four military strategic objectives, U.S. Armed Forces may be called upon to carry out eight missions: offensive operations, elimination, interdiction, active defense, passive defense, WMD consequence management, security cooperation and partner activities, and threat reduction cooperation. Capabilities development should address and prioritize the critical capability needs of these eight mission areas. *Offensive Operations* may include

EIGHT MISSION AREAS

Offensive Operations
Elimination Operations
Interdiction Operations
Active Defense
Passive Defense
WMD Consequence Management
Security Cooperation &
Partnership Activities
Threat Reduction Cooperation

kinetic and/or non-kinetic options (e.g., elements of space and information operations) to deter or defeat a WMD threat or subsequent use of WMD. *Elimination Operations* are operations systematically to locate, characterize,

secure, disable, and/or destroy a State or non-State actor's WMD programs and related capabilities. *Interdiction Operations* are designed to stop the proliferation of WMD, delivery systems, associated and dual-use technologies, materials, and expertise from transiting between States of concern and between State and non-State actors, whether undertaken by the military or by other agencies of government (e.g., law enforcement). *Active Defense* measures include, but are not limited to, missile defense (ballistic and cruise), air defense, special operations, and security operations to defend against conventionally and unconventionally delivered

WMD. *Passive Defense* includes measures to minimize or negate the vulnerability to and minimize effects of WMD use against U.S., partner, and allied Armed Forces as well as U.S. military interests, installations, and critical infrastructure. *Consequence Management* includes those actions taken to reduce the effects of a WMD attack or event, including Toxic Industrial Chemicals and Toxic Industrial Materials, and assist in the restoration of essential operations and services at home and abroad. U.S. Armed Forces must be prepared to support the response to a WMD event in the homeland and, when directed, support allies and partners. *Security Cooperation and Partner Activities* are those military activities that support international efforts to combat WMD. The military must strive to expand and exercise combating WMD partnerships with a goal of creating partners that can provide for themselves and assist during coalition operations. *Threat Reduction Cooperation* activities are those activities undertaken with the consent and cooperation of host nation authorities to enhance physical security; and emplace detection equipment; reduce, dismantle, redirect, and/or improve protection of a State's existing WMD programs, stockpiles, and capabilities.

Conclusion To ensure that the United States, its Armed Forces, allies, partners, and interests are neither threatened nor attacked by WMD, U.S. Armed Forces must be prepared to: defeat and deter WMD use and deter next use; protect from, respond to, and recover from WMD use; prevent, dissuade, or deny WMD proliferation or possession; and reduce, eliminate, or reverse WMD possession. We will accomplish these MSOs through eight combating WMD missions, all of which are supported by the strategic enablers.

Strategic Goal
Ensure that the United States, its Armed Forces, allies, partners, and interests are neither coerced nor attacked by enemies using WMD

End States
Standards by which we can measure effectiveness towards the Strategic Goal

Military Strategic Objectives
Defeat, Deter – Protect, Respond, Recover – Defend, Dissuade, Deny – Reduce, Destroy, Reverse

Strategic Enablers
Intelligence – Partnership Capacity – Strategic Communication Support

Eight Mission Areas
Offensive operations, Elimination, Interdiction, Active Defense, Passive Defense, WMD Consequence Management, Security Cooperation and Partner Activities, Threat Reduction Cooperation

CHAPTER 1
Introduction

> *"Weapons of mass destruction (WMD) — nuclear, biological and chemical — in the hands of hostile States and terrorists represent one of the greatest security challenges facing the United States...we cannot always be successful in preventing and containing the proliferation of WMD to hostile States and terrorists. Therefore, U.S. military and appropriate civilian agencies must possess the full range of operational capabilities to counter the threat and use of WMD by States and terrorists against the United States, U.S. military forces, and friends and allies."*
>
> The National Strategy to Combat WMD, December 2002

Purpose

The *National Military Strategy (NMS) to Combat Weapons of Mass Destruction (WMD)* is derived from the Department of Defense's (DOD) mission to dissuade, deter, and defeat those who seek to harm the United States, its allies, and partners through WMD use or threat of use and, if attacked, to mitigate the effects and restore deterrence. Its purpose is to provide DOD Components guidance and a strategic framework for combating WMD. The strategy uses an "ends, ways, means" approach to planning, executing and resourcing that emphasizes those combating WMD missions in which the military plays a prominent role.

21st Century WMD Security Environment

Over the past two decades, the global WMD threat has grown more complex and diverse, and it has broadened from a focus on State threats to one that includes both State and non-State actors. The WMD threat is not limited to a specific region or type of conflict. Our enemies are evolving and our strategy must be flexible and enable proactive measures. These actors will threaten the United States, its allies, and partners with the use of WMD. Non-State actors include terrorists, extremists, terrorist networks, transnational threats, non-governmental organizations, businesses, rogue scientist/ technicians, as well as individuals acting independently of any organization. Failed States or States in transition that cannot guarantee the security of their WMD pose additional challenges.

We will give top priority to dissuading, deterring, and defeating those who seek to harm the United States directly, especially extremist enemies with weapons of mass destruction. Non-State actors may be highly organized, networked, and aided by State sponsors of terrorism. Their efforts to develop or acquire WMD may be facilitated by criminal organizations, business enterprises, or international proliferation networks. The growing spread of technical expertise, materials, and sophisticated dual-use technology contributes to this challenge. These global proliferation activities employ a combination of secrecy, dispersion, and fiscal resources that must be located, monitored, and ultimately targeted. Other challenges include: acquisition and/or use of WMD by terrorist organizations against the United States; the deployment of medium- and longer-range ballistic missiles; cruise missiles and unmanned aerial vehicles; underground Chemical, Biological, Radiological, and Nuclear (CBRN), and missile-related facilities; the proliferation of WMD and related equipment and technologies from current and/or suspected nuclear weapons States to other nation-States of concern; and the poor security of existing CBRN materials.[1]

---

[1] DI-1569-43q-04, World Wide NBC and Proliferation Threat (Feb 04).

This security environment is complicated by the fact that our ability to detect, identify, and characterize WMD threats depends on effective intelligence collection, analysis and dissemination. States maintaining or seeking WMD may use creative means to conceal the status of their programs, and intelligence on non-State actors may be difficult to acquire. In addition, dual-use materials and technologies require novel approaches to intelligence activities. Although we will continue to improve our intelligence collection and analysis techniques, we must recognize that plans and decisions will need to be made with limited or incomplete WMD-related intelligence.

National Guidance

The National Security Strategy of the United States (NSS) sets forth an active strategy to counter transnational terror networks, rogue nations, and aggressive States that possess or are

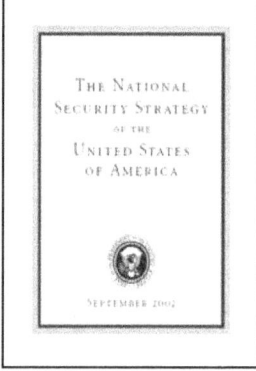

working to acquire WMD. It notes that the United States must advance this strategy through strengthened alliances, the establishment of new partnerships with former adversaries, innovative use of military forces, modern technologies, and increased emphasis on intelligence collection and analysis.

The National Strategy to Combat Weapons of Mass Destruction builds

on the National Security Strategy (NSS) and articulates a proactive and comprehensive strategy built upon the three pillars of nonproliferation, counterproliferation, and consequence management to counter the WMD threat in all of its dimensions. The *National Military Strategy to Combat WMD* supports this national framework by applying the three pillars across the spectrum of military operations. Recognizing that WMD in the hands of terrorists is one of the gravest threats facing the United States, a *Strategy for Combating WMD Terrorism* has also been developed among various Departments and Agencies in order to more fully coordinate activities across the government.

The National Defense Strategy of the United States of America (NDS)

also builds on the foregoing and outlines an active, layered approach to the defense of the nation and its interests. It highlights the nexus among terrorism, WMD proliferation, and problem States that possess or seek WMD. The *National Military Strategy to Combat*

WMD supports accomplishing the NDS objectives by applying its implementation guidelines to the challenges posed by WMD.

The National Military Strategy of the United States of America describes military objectives and joint operating concepts from which the Secretaries of the Military Departments and combatant commanders identify desired capabilities and against which the Chairman of the Joint Chiefs of Staff assesses risk. It calls for a responsive, joint force capable of protecting against WMD and defeating WMD-armed adversaries.

The *National Military Strategy to Combat WMD* builds on the combating WMD guidance in the Chairman's National Military Strategy by establishing strategic objectives and mission areas, and defining the guiding principles and strategic enablers for the military's role in combating WMD.

The National Military Strategic Plan for the War on Terrorism (NMSP-WOT) constitutes the comprehensive military plan to prosecute the Global War on Terrorism (GWOT) for the Armed Forces of the United States. This plan guides the contributions of the Combatant Commands, the Military Departments, Combat Support Agencies and Field Support Activities of the United States in protecting the United States and its interests abroad, defeating the terrorist extremist threat, and ultimately, establishing and maintaining a global environment inhospitable to terrorism. It identifies capabilities the Military Departments should provide, guides ongoing activities, identifies priorities, establishes a mechanism to measure progress, and informs planning for future DoD actions in the GWOT. One of the critical enablers of our national strategy for the war on terror is the prevention of terrorist possession or use of WMD against the United States, its allies,

partners, and interests. One of the six military strategic objectives listed in the NMSP-WOT deals specifically with Weapons of Mass Destruction. *Denying WMD proliferation, recovering and eliminating uncontrolled materials, and maintaining capacity for consequence management* are essential to ensuring our national security. Military activities include efforts to: detect and monitor acquisition and development; and conduct counterproliferation operations, security cooperation activities, WMD active and passive defense, and coordination of consequence management operations. These activities are fully compatible with the *National Military Strategy for Combating WMD.*

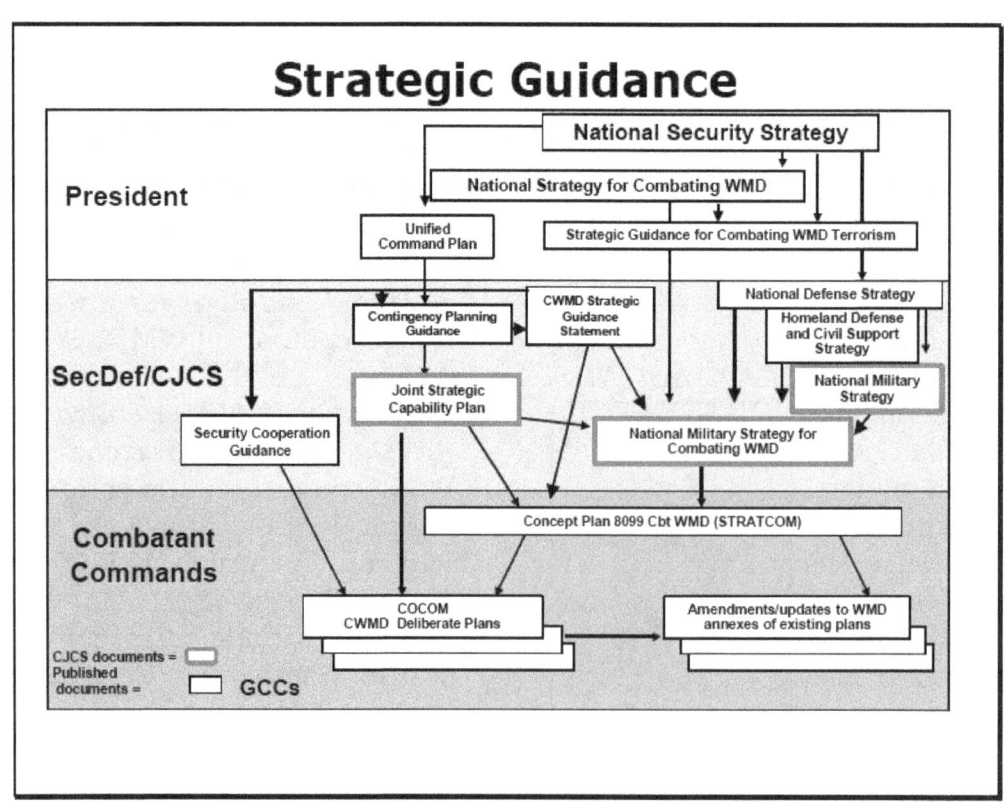

CHAPTER 2
Guiding Principles

Six guiding principles underpin the National Military Strategy to Combat WMD. These include developing an active and layered defense-in-depth, establishing integrated command and control, implementing global force management, utilizing capabilities-based planning, utilizing an effects-based approach, and assuring allies and partners. These principles should be used as a foundation for the development of all combating WMD concepts of operations and plans.

Active, Layered, Defense-in-Depth. In order to protect the United States and defeat aggressors, the U.S. Armed Forces must establish an active defense. U.S. Armed Forces will focus military planning, posture, operations, and capabilities, in accordance with mission essential tasks, on the active, forward and layered defense of our nation, our allies, partners, and interests. They will develop capabilities that support the spectrum of combating WMD missions with an emphasis on defeating threats as far from the United States as possible. U.S.

Six Guiding Principles

Active, Layered, Defense-in-Depth
Situational Awareness and Integrated
Command and Control
Global Force Management
Capabilities-Based Planning
Effects-Based Approach
Assurance

Armed Forces should balance, synchronize, and coordinate all military combating WMD capabilities development and operations. Use of this approach will ensure a strong and in-depth defense against WMD.

Situational Awareness and Integrated Command and Control. The decision to employ specialized combating WMD capabilities for simultaneous operations demands a highly flexible and adaptive command and control process informed by timely, credible, and actionable intelligence. Combating WMD intelligence is currently limited and, in the interim, planning and execution decisions must be made with limited and incomplete intelligence. The ability to share timely information among commanders, other U.S. Government agencies, our allies, and partners in a multi-layered security environment is essential to operational success in combating WMD. Senior leaders require common, timely, accurate and relevant information for decisions that affect resources, plans, and the employment of capabilities to combat WMD, some of which may be high-demand, low-density assets. Additionally, some time-sensitive situations, such as prosecution of fleeting targets and/or situations where speed of decision or action is critical to success, will require a streamlined planning and coordination process to develop courses of action rapidly and gain the necessary authorities for execution.

Global Force Management. An essential part of combating WMD is our ability to plan, posture, and deploy successfully and in a timely manner, and to sustain combating WMD forces. WMD specific capabilities must be part of our global force presence and must be fully visible to planners and decision makers through the global force management process. Forward presence, either permanently stationed or rotational, has key advantages in combating WMD. U.S. Armed Forces must be prepared to conduct traditional passive and active defense, as well as offensive operations, concurrently with the conduct of interdiction and elimination missions abroad, support of homeland security, and conduct of WMD consequence management. In some cases, WMD expertise may be provided via reach-back capability. Any combating WMD capabilities we develop in the future must be visible to combatant command planner and include responsive and agile forces that can be rapidly task-organized and

equipped to accomplish assigned missions.

Capabilities Based Planning. Because it is more important to possess effective capabilities to counter how adversaries may challenge us, rather than to know who those adversaries may be or where we might face them, U.S. Armed Forces must develop a broad spectrum of tools to counter these means and achieve desired effects. Capabilities-based plans for resourcing should focus on development of tools that have broad-spectrum application. For example, our planning and capability development should not be focused on one biological warfare threat agent, one threat country, or one non-State actor. We must plan for and develop capabilities that could be employed against a range of threats and associated capabilities while balancing the requirements for targeted strategies against known proliferators. Capabilities should be developed and deployed using an aggressive spiral development process providing military capabilities early and ensuring continuous upgrades to fielded capabilities (including forces) throughout their lifecycle.

Effects-Based Approach. We will use an effects-based approach in planning, execution, and assessments to achieve efficient results and reduce risk to mission and campaign objectives, as well as to our combating WMD-related resources. An effects-based approach to planning links plans and action to desired effects.

Combating WMD plans must reflect a synergistic and cumulative application of the eight mission areas (See Figure 2) at the tactical, operational, and strategic levels. Through this process planners identify the critical centers of gravity, linkages, and courses of action tied to probable enemy reactions. The effects-based approach produces plans and operations that allow commanders to accomplish assigned missions effectively and efficiently. Execution actions focus on critical centers of gravity to achieve the optimal effects using the minimal operational effort required to meet mission objectives. This efficient application of force is critical to combating WMD operations. The best operational outcome is one that achieves desired effects on the adversary while minimizing the adversaries' effectiveness against us.

Assurance. We must seek to solidify and enable the active support of international allies and partners to realize the goals of our comprehensive combating WMD strategy. Using the tools of routine dialogue, military-to-military contacts, burden-sharing arrangements, and combined military activities enabled by our operations by the regional Combatant Commands, we assure and build allied and partner will and capacity for combined action. Where possible, we will encourage action by like-minded States, work with our international allies and partners, and operate through regional States to combat WMD actively. Combating WMD plans and activities will incorporate specific activities to encourage and enable this allied and coalition participation. We will fulfill our alliance and other defense commitments, help protect our common interests, and develop training and capabilities that contribute to combating WMD.

CHAPTER 3
Strategic Military Framework

The strategic military framework to combat WMD (Figure 1) consists of ends (the military strategic goal and associated end state), ways (military strategic objectives), and means (combatant commands, Military Departments, and combat support agencies) applied across the three pillars of the National Strategy to Combat WMD (nonproliferation, counterproliferation, and consequence management).

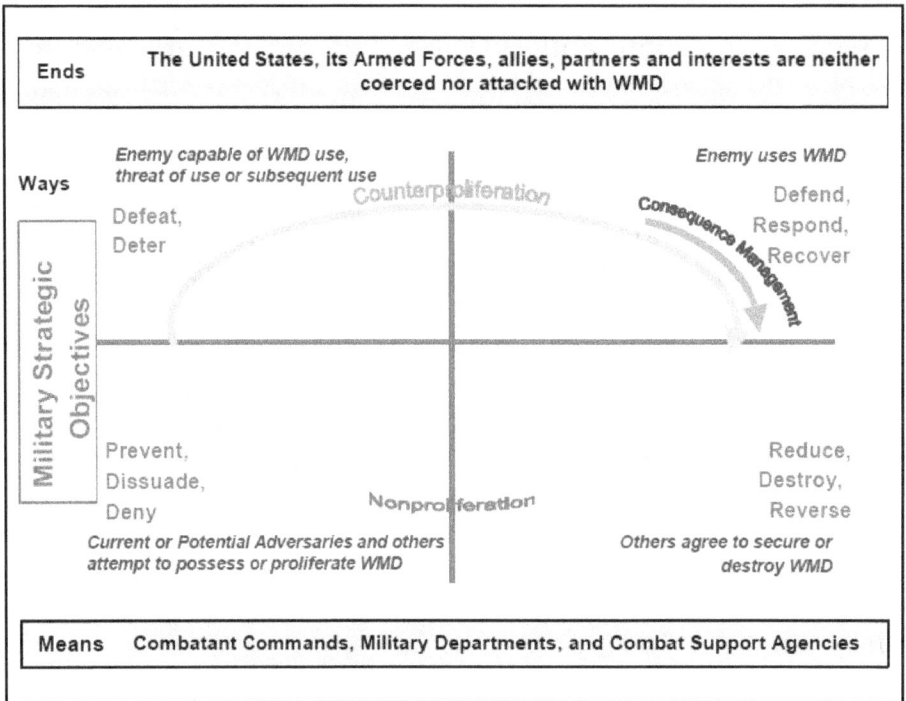

Figure 1 – Strategic Military Framework

Ends (Military Strategic Goal and Associated Endstates)

Our military strategic goal is to ensure that the United States, its Armed Forces, allies, partners, and interests are neither coerced nor attacked with WMD. Specific end states delineate standards by which we can measure our effectiveness:

1. U.S. Armed Forces, in concert with other elements of U.S. national power, deter WMD use.

2. U. S. Armed Forces are prepared to defeat an adversary threatening to use WMD and prepared to deter follow-on use.

3. Existing worldwide WMD are secure, and the U.S. Armed Forces contribute, as

appropriate, to secure, reduce, reverse or eliminate it.

4. Current or potential adversaries are dissuaded from producing WMD.

5. Current or potential adversaries' WMD are detected and characterized and elimination is sought.

6. Proliferation of WMD and related materials to current and/or potential adversaries is dissuaded, prevented, defeated or reversed.

7. If WMD are used against the United States or its interests, U.S. Armed Forces are capable of minimizing the effects in order to continue operations in a WMD environment and assist U.S. civil authorities, allies and partners.

8. U.S. Armed Forces assist in attributing the source of attack, respond decisively, and/or deter future attacks.

9. Allies, partners, and U.S. civilian agencies are capable partners in combating WMD.

Ways (Military Strategic Objectives)

The military strategic objectives (MSOs) outlined below describe how the U.S. Armed Forces will accomplish its strategic goal. The MSOs are achieved through eight missions conducted across the combating WMD continuum. These missions are guided in turn by six

principles that underpin the *National Military Strategy to Combat WMD*. These guiding principles, the eight mission areas, and their strategic enablers are discussed in Chapter 4.

Military Strategic Objectives

Defeat, Deter
Protect, Respond, Recover
Defend, Dissuade, Deny
Reduce, Destroy, Reverse

Defeat and Deter WMD use and subsequent use. The purpose of this objective is to counter an adversary capable of and willing to use WMD. The Department of Defense will further develop military capabilities to eliminate WMD threats in a non-permissive environment. Our intent and actions should deter a potential adversary from considering the initial or subsequent use of WMD. Adversaries must believe they will suffer severe consequences and that their objectives will be denied if they threaten or resort to the use of WMD. Deterrence of WMD in the current era requires that U.S. Armed Forces possess a broad set of military capabilities to prevent an adversary from attacking with WMD and to protect against attacks. In order to deter an adversary's use of WMD and to defeat its WMD capability when deterrence fails, U.S. Armed Forces may be called upon to conduct offensive operations, elimination operations, interdiction operations, or active defense.

Defend, Respond and Recover from WMD use. This purpose of this objective is to respond to an adversary that has used WMD on the battlefield or against strategic U. S. interests. Although our primary focus is to minimize the effects of WMD on military operations, U.S. Armed Forces must be prepared to support the response to a WMD event in the homeland and, when directed, support allies and partners. Despite the best efforts of the United States, our allies, and partners, it is possible that our adversaries might successfully attack with WMD. To defend against and recover from WMD use, U.S. Armed Forces will execute passive defense measures and be prepared to conduct WMD consequence management activities.

Prevent, Dissuade or Deny WMD proliferation or possession. The purpose of this objective is to keep WMD out of the hands of adversaries and potential adversaries, while simultaneously increasing ally and partner capability and support for combating WMD activities. Current and potential adversaries might believe that possession and/or proliferation of WMD, delivery systems, and related materials is a possible way to impose their will on the United States, its allies, or partners. To prevent, dissuade or deny adversaries or potential adversaries from possessing or proliferating WMD, U.S. Armed Forces will be prepared to conduct offensive operations. The military must also support interdiction efforts, security cooperation, and nonproliferation efforts. In addition, we will take actions to assure allies and partners that they do not need to possess WMD.

Reduce, Destroy, or Reverse WMD possession. The purpose of this objective is to destroy or secure WMD when there is an agreement to do so. Current and potential allies and partners might desire to give up possession of WMD or associated technology at any point on the development or deployment spectrum. To reverse WMD programs and reduce WMD and related material stockpiles, the U. S. Armed Forces will support threat reduction cooperation as well as be prepared to assist in cooperative stockpile destruction activities.

Means (Combatant Commands, Military Departments, and Combat Support Agencies)

The combatant commands, Military Departments, and combat support agencies are the means to accomplish MSOs. The combatant commands are primarily responsible for planning and execution; the Military Departments are primarily responsible for organizing, training, and equipping; and combat support agencies support both the combatant commands and the Military Departments.

Commander, United States Strategic Command (CDRUSSTRATCOM) is the lead combatant commander for integrating and synchronizing DOD efforts in combating WMD. Consistent with this assignment, USSTRATCOM will integrate and synchronize applicable Department of Defense-wide efforts across the doctrine, organization, training, material, leadership, personnel, and facilities spectrum. Combatant Commanders will continue to execute combating WMD missions within their AORs. The Military Departments develop doctrine and organize, train, and equip their forces to combat WMD unless otherwise directed. The agencies provide specialized capabilities and expertise in support of Combatant Commander execution of combating WMD missions. In addition, Commander, U.S. Northern Command (CDRUSNORTHCOM) and Commander, U.S. Pacific Command (CDRUSPACOM) have unique responsibilities for supporting domestic WMD consequence management activities.

Combating WMD is a full-spectrum, multi-faceted mission set that will fully challenge DOD and require effective cooperation among U.S. Government agencies, international allies and partners. WMD proliferation is a global threat and must be addressed with a broad array of capabilities. Military efforts will need to be integrated with other organizations and nations that possess capabilities, resources, or information that can contribute to the mission. In general, the demands across the full spectrum of combating WMD will require the military to work closely with domestic agencies, allies, and partners to dissuade, deter, and defeat those who seek to harm us with WMD. Precluding the convergence of WMD and terrorism requires, in great part, coordinating combating WMD objectives with the objectives of the Global War on Terrorism, as described in the *National Strategy for Combating WMD Terrorism*. We must reinforce technical and logistical barriers to WMD acquisition and develop plans and capabilities for interdiction where necessary. Finally, we must be prepared to prevent – through force if necessary – nation States from supporting or facilitating WMD acquisition and/or use by terrorists.

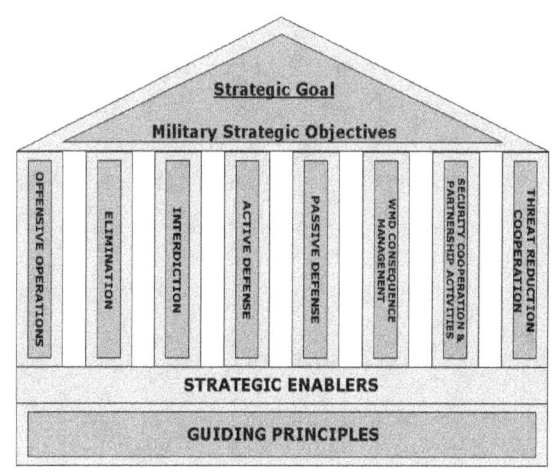

CHAPTER 4
Operational Guidance

Strategic Enablers

Strategic enablers are crosscutting capabilities that facilitate execution of the military strategy. They enhance the effectiveness and integration of military combating WMD mission capabilities. Commanders must continually assess enabling capabilities and identify required improvements. Three enablers facilitate DOD's efforts to combat WMD: intelligence, partnership capacity, and strategic communication.

Intelligence. Intelligence directly supports strategy, planning, and decision-making; facilitates improvements in operational capabilities; and informs programming and risk management. WMD intelligence is a supporting enabler of all eight mission areas. Since we recognize the limits of combating WMD intelligence, planning and execution decisions will be made using limited or incomplete information. However, we can strengthen our current WMD intelligence by improving our capacity for early warning of CBRN attack; transforming organizations and processes to improve combating WMD intelligence support; and fusing operations and intelligence to improve collection, assessment, and dissemination of intelligence. Without actionable intelligence, we are unable to prevent, defeat, or reverse the proliferation and/or use of WMD. Understanding the WMD capabilities of potential adversaries is essential. An accurate and complete understanding of the full range of WMD threats, proliferation activities, and trends is vital to developing effective near and long-term approaches. To reduce uncertainty, our intelligence capability must exploit a variety of sources, facilitate information sharing, and improve situational awareness.

Strategic ☐☐ablers

☐☐te☐☐☐ence
Partners☐ip ☐apacity
☐trate☐ic ☐b☐☐☐unication ☐upport

Detection is an essential aspect of combating WMD intelligence. It is the ability to "see" the threat. Detection affects decision making in each of the eight mission areas at the strategic, operational, and tactical levels. Detection ranges from intelligence community efforts to collect information necessary for strategic planning, investment, and decision making to operational or tactical detection of a CBRN threat on the battlefield. Detection also encompasses the capability to attribute the source of a CBRN attack or impending attack in order to deter future actions. Early detection enables the intelligence community to characterize the nature of WMD facilities and inform decision makers of various defeat options more effectively.

Partnership Capacity. Building partnership capacity bilaterally and multilaterally enhances our capability to combat WMD. Incorporating our partners' and allies' combating WMD capabilities supports our ability to defend the homeland, deter forward, and conduct multiple, simultaneous activities. We must assist international partners to build capacities to combat WMD effectively. Security cooperation efforts should not only, for example, focus on missile defense cooperation or the Proliferation Security Initiative (PSI), but should equally stress passive defense, elimination, and WMD consequence management cooperation, including efforts in multilateral fora. Incorporating such combating WMD cooperation into current Combatant Command Theater security cooperation initiatives should empower other nations and reduce potential burdens on the United States. Given the potential for operating in a WMD environment in the future, it is critical that partner and allied nations have the ability not only to survive an attack, but also to eliminate further threats and restore essential operations and military departments. Assistance from the international community could become a force multiplier in the U.S. effort to sustain operations and to combat WMD effectively.

Strategic Communication Support. Strategic communication complements combating WMD efforts and helps shape perceptions at the global, regional, and national levels. The military plays a significant supporting role in the larger U.S. Government effort to communicate and demonstrate our resolve. Making progress requires the effective integration of diplomacy, public affairs, and information operations. Strategic communications shape perceptions at the global, regional, and national levels. U.S. words and actions reassure allies and partners and underscore, to potential adversaries, the costs and risks associated with WMD acquisition and use.

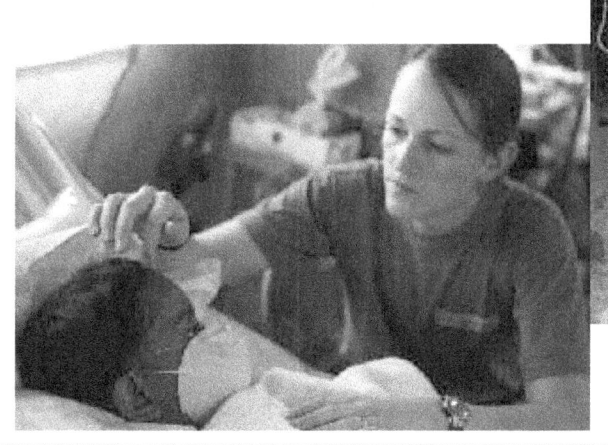

Military Mission Areas

The military mission is to dissuade, deter, defend, and defeat those who seek to harm the United States, its allies, and its partners through WMD use or threat of use and, if attacked, mitigate the effects and restore deterrence. This mission is in direct support of the three pillars (non-proliferation, counterproliferation, and consequence management) of the *National Strategy for Combating WMD*.

As U.S. Armed Forces develop plans and capabilities using the guiding principles articulated above, they should focus on the four MSOs. Across these objectives, U.S. Armed Forces may be called upon to carry out eight missions (see Figure 2): offensive operations, elimination, interdiction, active defense, passive defense, WMD consequence management, security cooperation and partner activities, and threat reduction cooperation. Capabilities development should address and prioritize the critical capability needs of the eight mission areas.

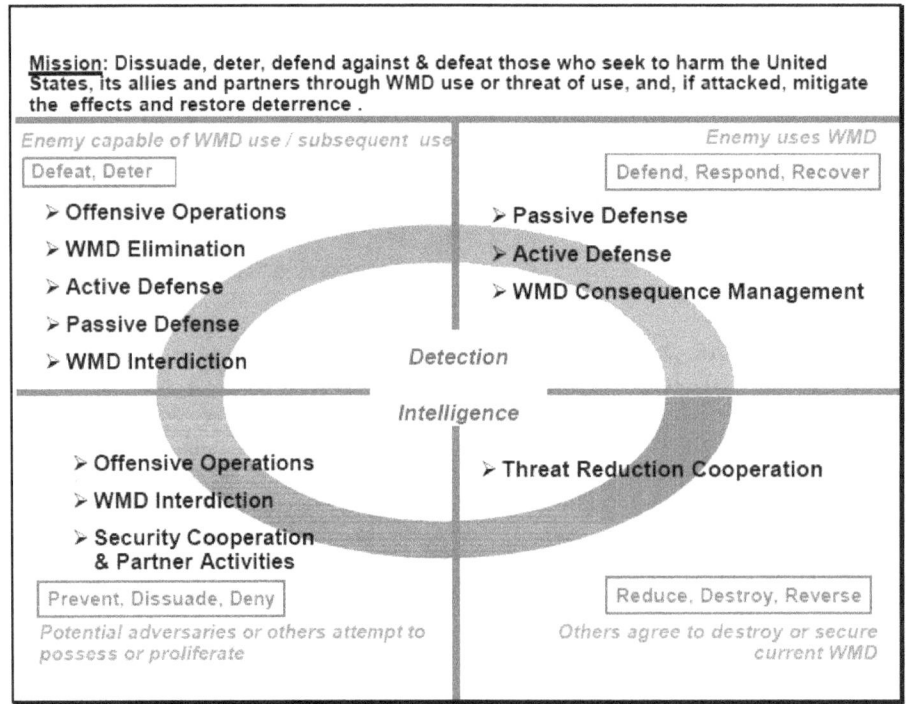

Figure 2 – Military Mission Areas

Offensive Operations.
Offensive operations may include kinetic (both conventional and nuclear) and/or non-kinetic options (e.g., information operations) to deter or defeat a WMD threat or subsequent use of WMD. Offensive operations encompass the detection, identification, disruption, and/or destruction of an adversary's WMD assets, means of delivery, associated facilities and other high-value targets necessary to achieve the desired effects and objectives. Offensive operations may be conducted at any time, across the spectrum of conflict. Defeating some types of targets requires specialized capabilities and operational concepts, including the capability to locate, seize, secure, render safe, recapture, recover, and/or destroy lost or stolen WMD; the capability to defeat hard and deeply buried targets; the capability to defeat or neutralize the chemical or biological agent and associated weapons and equipment with little to no collateral effect; and the capacity to find, fix, track, target, engage, and assess (F2T2EA) attacks against WMD targets. Each link and node in the proliferation pathway has vulnerabilities; we must have the plans and capabilities to exploit these vulnerabilities and affect each node through kinetic or non-kinetic means.

Elimination Operations.
WMD Elimination operations are operations to systematically locate, characterize, secure, disable, and/or destroy a State or non-State actor's WMD programs and related capabilities in hostile or uncertain environments. Elimination operations may be required when offensive operations against WMD targets carry unacceptable risk to the civilian population or U. S. and partner/allied armed forces.

The priority for elimination activities is to reduce or eliminate the threat to the United States and to support military and national objectives. Operational planning and execution for elimination must ensure the safety of U.S. and partner/allied armed forces through 1) security operations to prevent the looting or capture of WMD and related materials; and 2) rendering harmless or destroying of weapons, materials, agents, and delivery systems that pose an immediate or direct threat to U.S. Armed Forces and the civilian population. Intelligence exploitation of program experts, documents, and other media as well as previously secured weapons and material is essential to combating further WMD proliferation and to prevent regeneration of a WMD capability. Once these activities have been accomplished, elimination operations may be transferred, if directed, to other U. S. Government agencies, international agencies, or host nations to continue destruction of WMD programs and to redirect and monitor dual-use industry and expertise capable of regenerating WMD capability.

DOD must develop, institutionalize, and exercise a joint capability to eliminate WMD in uncertain environments. This will require integrating the elimination mission into doctrine, organization, training, personnel and education, material, leadership, and programming processes. Commanders should be prepared to conduct elimination activities from the initiation of operations until it is determined that a transfer of authority to another agency is warranted.

Interdiction Operations. WMD Interdiction operations are designed to stop the transit of WMD, delivery systems, associated and dual-use technologies, materials, and expertise between States of concern and between State and non-State actors, whether undertaken by the military or by other agencies of government (e.g., law enforcement). Commanders must be ready to interdict WMD and related materials in both non-permissive and permissive environments and coordinate efforts with other U.S. Government agencies and partner/ allied States, as directed.

For example commanders should prepare to intercept, identify, safely secure, and dispose or render-safe any materials suspected as WMD-related, as directed. The focus of interdiction must extend beyond traditional military interdiction conducted during hostilities to encompass peacetime military interdiction of dual-use materials. These operations to interdict proliferation-related shipments assist in the disruption and dismantlement of proliferation networks. Commanders must ensure the capability to divert, disrupt, delay, or destroy the enemy's WMD capability, in both permissive and non-permissive environments, before it can be used against U.S. Armed Forces. A systematic interagency approach is required to respond to the growing volume and complexity of the WMD trade. Without a sustained effort to track and disrupt this trade, the United States, its allies, and partners may miss critical opportunities to deny access to WMD. U.S. Armed Forces must continue to enhance interdiction capability to stop the proliferation of WMD and related materials. This mission is particularly dependent on timely, credible, and actionable intelligence.

The emphasis on interdiction of WMD-related trafficking in a permissive environment has been highlighted by the United States participation in the Proliferation Security Initiative (PSI). In support of the PSI, a growing number of like-minded nations are planning, exercising, and executing interdiction operations aimed at disrupting trafficking in WMD, their delivery systems, and related materials. The PSI represents a political commitment by the United States and others to undertake WMD-related interdiction through a variety of means (including military), both nationally and, when necessary, in cooperation with other partners. In many cases PSI activities will involve U.S. Government agencies and international partners that may not be familiar with U.S. military planning and exercise procedures, requiring commands to adjust to meet the unique requirements of these exercises and operations.

Active Defense. WMD Active defense measures include, but are not limited to, missile defense (ballistic and cruise), air defense, special operations, and security operations to defend against conventionally and unconventionally delivered WMD. A layered, networked defensive capability will incorporate networked homeland

and regional land, sea, air, and space-based systems, and will employ both kinetic and non-kinetic means of defeating the delivery of WMD.

Passive Defense. WMD Passive defense includes measures to minimize or negate the vulnerability and minimize effects of WMD use against U.S. and partner/allied forces, as well as U.S. military interests, installations, and critical infrastructure. Passive defense operations are addressed extensively in Joint and Military Department doctrine, and are organized around four key capabilities:

- **Sense** – The ability to provide continuous information about the CBRN situation.
- **Shape** – The ability to characterize CBRN hazards to understand the current situation and predict future events.
- **Shield** – The ability to protect from the hazard.
- **Sustain** – The ability to continue to operate in a contaminated environment.

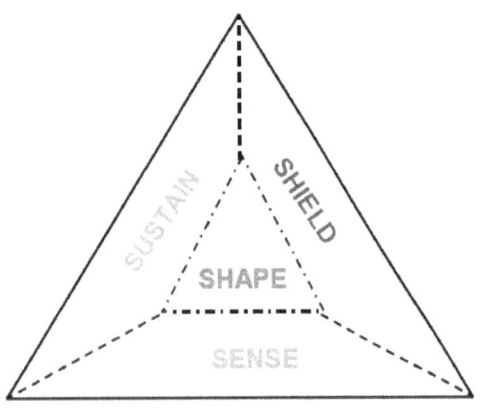

Success in passive defense operations depends on the effective integration of equipment, trained personnel, and proven techniques, tactics, and procedures. In addition, passive defense capabilities contribute to the success of other combating WMD missions, including interdiction, elimination, and consequence management.

WMD Consequence Management. WMD consequence management includes those actions taken to reduce the effects of a WMD attack or event, including Toxic Industrial Chemicals (TIC) and Toxic Industrial Materials (TIM), and assist in the restoration of essential operations and services at home and abroad. U.S. Armed Forces must be prepared to support the response to a WMD event in the homeland and, when directed, support allies and partners.

At home, U.S. Armed Forces may be required to support consequence management efforts of the Federal Government. When directed or authorized by the President, the Secretary of Defense may authorize Defense Support of Civil Authorities (DSCA). Abroad, when requested by a host nation, the President may authorize and the Secretary of Defense may direct DoD support to U. S. Government foreign consequence management operations. For all consequence management activities, the military must be prepared either to support or lead consequence management operations, as directed.

Security Cooperation and Partner Activities. Combating WMD is a global challenge, and it requires a coordinated international response. Security cooperation and partner activities are those military activities that support international efforts to combat WMD. These activities should promote improved partnership capacity to combat WMD across the eight mission areas. Examples of excellent progress to date include international participation in PSI activities, establishment of the NATO CBRN defense battalion, and development of a NATO elimination capability. The military must strive to expand and exercise combating WMD partnerships with a goal of creating partners that can provide for themselves and assist during coalition operations across the eight mission areas.

U.S. Armed Forces should undertake cooperative activities with regional military partners that promote improved partnership capacity to combat WMD. These activities should foster common threat awareness, coalition building, and interoperability.

visibility into these efforts to ensure theater security cooperation plans and security measures are consistent with threat reduction initiatives.

Military support to nonproliferation efforts are those activities that assist U.S. and international efforts to prevent, dissuade, or deny State and non-State actors access to WMD-relevant capabilities. Military activities include support to international activities including support for implementation of treaties, agreements, sanctions and export control regimes and frameworks, and national, international, and host-nation programs.

Threat Reduction Cooperation. Threat reduction cooperation activities are those activities undertaken with the consent and cooperation of host nation authorities to enhance physical security; emplace detection equipment; and reduce, dismantle, redirect, and/or improve protection of a State's existing WMD programs, stockpiles and capabilities. The military must be prepared to provide support for these missions once approved by the Secretary of Defense. Although not primarily a combatant commander responsibility, combatant commanders must maintain

Chapter 5
Conclusion

To ensure that the United States, its Armed Forces, allies, partners, and interests are neither threatened nor attacked by WMD, U.S. Armed Forces must be prepared to: defeat and deter WMD use and deter next use; defend against, respond to, and recover from WMD use; prevent, dissuade, or deny WMD proliferation or possession; and reduce, eliminate, or reverse WMD possession. We will accomplish these MSOs through eight combating WMD missions: offensive operations, elimination, interdiction, active defense, passive defense, consequence management, security cooperation and partner activities, and threat reduction cooperation.

As U.S. Armed Forces develop plans to conduct the combating WMD missions, six principles should guide our actions: an active, layered defense-in-depth; integrated command and control; global force management; capabilities-based planning; effects-based approach; and assurance. In addition, Combatant Commanders must continually assess and recommend improvements for the strategic enablers of intelligence/detection capabilities, partnership capacity, and strategic communication support. Appropriately organized and resourced, this strategy will effectively balance military and strategic risk over the long term. It will enable us to combat the WMD threats of today and transform the Joint Force to address the WMD challenges of tomorrow.

Annex A—Terms and Definitions

Active Defense. Military measures to prevent, deter, or defeat the delivery of WMD. Measures include offensive and defensive, conventional or unconventional actions to detect, divert, and destroy an adversary's WMD and/or delivery means while en route to their target. (This term and its definition are applicable only in the context of this publication and cannot be referenced outside this publication.)

Combating WMD (CWMD). The integrated and dynamic activities of the Department of Defense across the full range of counterproliferation, nonproliferation, and consequence management efforts to counter WMD, their means of delivery, and related materials.

Counterproliferation (CP). Actions to defeat the threat or use of weapons of mass destruction against the United States, U.S. Armed Forces, its allies, and partners.

Elimination. Military operations to systematically locate, characterize, secure, disable, and/or destroy a State or non-State actor's WMD programs and related capabilities in hostile or uncertain environments. (This term and its definition are applicable only in the context of this publication and cannot be referenced outside this publication.)

Interdiction. Operations to stop the transit of WMD, delivery systems and associated technologies, materials and expertise between States, and between State and non-State actors of proliferation concern in any environment. (This term and its definition are applicable only in the context of this publication and cannot be referenced outside this publication.)

Nonproliferation (NP). Actions to prevent the proliferation of weapons of mass destruction by dissuading or impeding access to, or distribution of, sensitive technologies, material, and expertise.

Non-permissive environment. An operational environment in which host government forces, whether opposed to or receptive to operations that a unit intends to conduct, do not have effective control of the territory and population in the intended operational area (Uncertain Environment), OR an operational environment in which hostile forces have control as well as the intent and capability to oppose or react effectively to the operations a unit intends to conduct (Hostile Environment).

Offensive Operations. Kinetic (both conventional and nuclear) and/or non-kinetic operations to defeat, neutralize or deter a WMD threat or subsequent use of WMD. (This term and its definition are applicable only in the context of this publication and cannot be referenced outside this publication.)

Passive Defense. Measures to minimize or negate the vulnerability and effects of WMD employed against U.S. and partner/allied Armed Forces, as well as U.S. military interests, installations, and critical infrastructure. (This term and its definition are applicable only in the context of this publication and cannot be referenced outside this publication.)

Permissive Environment. Operational environment in which host country military and law enforcement agencies have control as well as the intent and capability to assist operations that a unit intends to conduct.

Proliferation. The transfer of WMD, related materials, technology, and expertise from suppliers to hostile States, or non-State actors.

Security Cooperation and Partner Activities. Activities to improve partner and allied capacity to combat WMD across the eight mission areas through military-to-military contact, burden sharing arrangements, combined military activities, and support to international activities.

Toxic Industrial Chemicals (TIC). Any chemical substance that can render forces ineffective under normal mission-oriented protective posture conditions. Primarily an inhalation hazard, but forces can receive a dosage through ingestions or absorption through the skin. NOTE: "Toxic industrial chemicals" is implied within the general discussion of the term "chemical agents," but this term does not apply within the definition of "Chemical Warfare Agents" due to their dual-use capability.

Toxic Industrial Materials (TIM). Any substance that, in a given quantity, produces toxic effect in exposed personnel through inhalation, ingestion, or absorption.

Threat Reduction Cooperation. Activities undertaken with the consent and cooperation of host nation authorities to enhance physical security, and to reduce, dismantle, redirect, and/or improve protection of a State's existing WMD program, stockpiles, and capabilities.

Weapons of Mass Destruction (WMD). Weapons that are capable of a high order of destruction and/or of being used in a manner so as to destroy large numbers of people. Weapons of mass destruction can be nuclear, biological, chemical, and radiological weapons, but exclude means of delivery of weapons where such means is a separable and divisible part of the weapon.

WMD Consequence Management. Actions taken to mitigate the effects of a WMD attack or event and restore essential operations and services at home and abroad. (This term and its definition are applicable only in the context of this publication and cannot be referenced outside this publication.)